Dude, where did your money go?

Brasília

2019

Dude, where did your money go?
Copyright © 2019
Aigo Pyles



**Proofreading**
Thais Teixeira Monteiro

**Translator**
Aline Barbosa Silva Vieira

**Graphic design and layout**
José Carlos S. Junior

**Cover**
José Carlos S. Junior

**1st Edition:** March 2019

The texts in the biblical references were extracted from the New International Version, unless otherwise specified.

**ISBN**: 978-85-5963-061-9

# SUMMARY

# PROLOGUE

At the time the New Testament Scriptures were written there were, at least, in those areas, two very common schools of thought: the Greek and Hebrew. There are many differences in the bases of these two schools, but one particular came to my understanding while I read this precious book; it is how they relate the spiritual and natural lives.

According to the Greek, the spiritual life was disconnected from the natural life, so faith was devoid from any action. A person could devote their faith to something and act completely different. Deceiving a person that you said you loved, for example, was not a contradiction for the Greek. It may seem crazy, but it's true. The Hebrew thought goes the other way. For Jews or Christians, the spiritual life is so connected to the natural life that there isn't any possibility to separate them; everything is spiritual and, at the same time, everything is natural.

Sadly, some of us don't think about how much the fundaments of the Greek thought have been rooted in the world and, consequently, might be present in the thought structure of some sons of God. Such thought has led to a dead faith, an expectation in God's promises and prosperity, but that never comes true. This book, however, presents us the spiritual life intertwined to the natural life, that is, prosperity not being a fruit of a "workless faith." The author developed, in his book, a clear vision of the "natural-spiritual" practical challenges that are necessary for us to reach a healthy prosperity. He didn't only give us subsidies of faith, using the Word of God, but also showed us the many practical paths connected to faith, providing us with a wide possibility of ways to prosper in our lives.

Still, two important aspects must be included here. One is related to how serious the subject brought by the author is; and the other is how this book was written in such a timely manner to the audience the author intended to reach.

Fear of God above everything, the responsibility of having resources, caution when handling money, Mammon's skill to seduce, the possibility of losing your heart to wealth, the seductions of luxury, the practice of consumerism, debt, savings, and the challenge of generosity are subjects that provide density to this book; dealing with money it's not child's play. It is for men and women of God who are conscious of God's eternal purpose. And this is approached through the author's stories and experiences. Such experiences may make us laugh, but at other times, they make us gasp, and they awaken us, encourage us, and if we are at the edge of an abyss, save us! The chapters are short, easy to read, but powerfully efficient in making us think, change, believe, and practice.

Lastly, time is key in this book. Not only the time in which the book is being published but the time of life in which the book will be read, which is youth. Wouldn't that be the best time to learn how to prosper? Wouldn't that be the best time to learn to be an entrepreneur, to be trained by a prosperous Father? The young reader, through this book, can anticipate great learning from adulthood which, most times, is learned at irreparable and irreversible costs. Have an open heart for this book, as well as a young heart. The content of this book will far exceed your expectations, leading you to greater wealth!

Pr. André Matias

# INTRODUCTION

I want to talk to you, young reader, and why not? You have your whole life ahead of you; you dream, make plans, and all the time, you're wondering, *What is my adulthood going to be like?*

Well, I remember when I was 10 years old, I wanted to work, earn money, so that I could buy the things that I wanted. I always asked my mom, my eternal role model for wisdom and discipline, "Mom, I want to work, I want to buy a BMX bike." Those who are older than 40 years old remember these. I used to daydream about it, I thought of the day I would be able to go to "Pitdog," which is what we call street burger stands in Goias, to eat a burger and maybe go to that nice restaurant called Pigali, which was nothing but a bowling alley that served pizza.

Sweet childhood; my aspirations were low, but these were the real desires of a 10-year-old.

That was when things started changing in my life. My mom and my dad got divorced, I didn't see my dad as often as I used to - he lived in Maranhao and had farms in Para. He was a rich man, but not prosperous and powerful in our reality. My mom, my sisters, and I lived in a small town in the state of Goias called Anapolis. At that time, my dad used to always come to visit us, every six months, and every time he was there, my mom asked him to stay at home with us. Even though he had another family, my mother always treated him kindly and even made his favorite dessert – a condensed milk flan, which was unlike any other, a true delicacy.

At the time, it was hard to assimilate, but one day, when the financial struggles arose – yes, they did, our father no longer lived with us and my mother had retired from her job at the bank, where she worked with my father for many years – my mother found herself in a difficult situation. My sisters and I went to good private schools at the time; my oldest sisters studied at a Catholic school called Auxilium, and I was on my 4th grade at an elementary school near my house.

We had to readjust to the reality of my mother's income. At that time, my two sisters had to study at a public school close to home, and I earned a scholarship at JK School. However, we still had to pay for part of the tuition. That was when I called my dad and he told me this: "Do you need money to pay for your school?" My answer was "yes." And he said, "Then find a way to get it yourself!" I am sure that at that moment he was just acting out of impulse and emotion, since he and my mom were going through tough times.

Wow!! That was hard to swallow. It hurt so much to know that I was on my own. But the truth is that I wasn't alone; I had a family who loved me and a God who never forgot about me.

I took this pain and took out the "best" that it could offer me. I did look for a way to get this money by myself.

That was when I had the brilliant idea of trading my soapbox derby for a shoe-shine kit. That was my first endeavor. At the age of 10, I had already become a small entrepreneur. I was excited, and I put on my best sneakers, some white Adidas with three blue lateral stripes, my soccer shorts (it was 1984), my best shirt, and off I went. With the shoe-shine box on my back, I went up Goias Avenue, in Anápolis, and I stood next to a bus stop that took people to Fabril, a district with a large slaughterhouse. Later, this slaughterhouse would become globally known as JBS-Friboi.

So there I was at the bus stop when I saw my first "victim"—well, my first client. With all of my expertise as a new entrepreneur, I approached the subject. I offered him my services and, surprisingly, he said yes! And now I was facing my first business lesson: learn what you're doing first. I didn't know how to shine shoes, but I thought, *How hard can it be? It's just a shoe, right?* Wrong. And that was when I realized it was much harder than I thought: the man was wearing white socks. Oh Lord… what do you do after you stain white socks with black grease? Obviously, I tucked his socks inside his shoes and finished up the service. And the best part was he even paid me for that.

I was done and I thought, *this is much easier than I thought.* Oh, sweet illusion! I was about to face my second lesson: competition is fierce, and at that stop, there was what we know in the business world as a cartel! The owners of that spot came up and asked me, "What are you doing here?" I, as always, a very polite boy, promptly replied, "It's none of your business!"

They literally *kicked* and punched me out of the bus stop.

There was my third lesson: always research about the market before getting into unknown waters.

I left, feeling very disappointed, and I came back home with some scratches and bruises on my legs. Do you remember when I told you I wasn't alone? God had already set everything up for me! I got home and told my story, and I almost gave my mother a heart attack. She then told that story to our neighbors, and do you know what happened? Of course, they felt bad for me and, starting with my brother-in-law, everyone gave me a job for a while. This was another valuable lesson – advertising is key.

I want to, through some of my funny experiences and stories, motivate you, young reader, to take some actions that can change and revolutionize *your* life story. Of course, we are a product of our environment, and your first environment is your family. Maybe you haven't learned many things from your parents, such as physics, chemistry, and biology, but I'm sure that you learned many other things that made you who you are today.

And this can be used by you to change the future of your children, grandchildren, and great-grandchildren. The book of wisdom in Proverbs makes it very clear when it teaches that a good man leaves an inheritance for the children of their children, so how about you leave a much better inheritance than money? How about you leave knowledge? Think about it; you can sow lettuce today and reap it very quickly, or you can choose to plant olive trees and reap them in 10, 20, 30 years from now, letting them stay in your house for hundreds of years. We are always sowing something, you just need to choose the right seeds.

I hope this book helps you choose the right seed for each moment because – as I learned from a great man of God – the right thing at the wrong time is the wrong thing. So choose the right seed wisely at the right time and fill your granaries not just with financial resources, but good experiences, friendships, and lessons that can linger for many generations. Be the driving force that changes the history of your life and the lives of those who you can influence. Have a great read!

# Chapter 1

# MY FIRST BICYCLE

The shoes soon were left behind, and now I was almost 11 years old, and I was convinced that I wanted to buy a BMX. Since I couldn't convince my dad to give me that bike, I talked to my mother; she would satisfy my heart's desires, right? Wrong. The budget was tight, and this guy that I had no idea who he was kept on getting in my way – Mr. Superfluous. How horrible! We only had enough money for our basic needs, and Mr. Superfluous was always stopping me from buying what I wanted. But a mother's love is endless, and so was my stubbornness. That was when she had a brilliant idea: we had two fans in our garage; those big fans you found inside the banks – of course, at that time, air conditioning was rare. My mother told me, "We have two fans, why don't you sell them and buy the bike?" Wow, I was excited, ecstatic, and I started thinking, *but to whom am I going to sell these fans?*

That was when, on a very hot Sunday, we were at the Anapolis Pentecostal Renewed Presbyterian Church, and *I thought, I know! Pastor Joel do Prado... I'm sure the church needs fans, no one can stand the heat!* So I gathered some courage and spoke to the pastor. This time, I had more experience; I knew how to conduct market research, so I saw a need and went straight to the point.

"Pastor Joel, how are you?" He greeted me with his usual cordiality. I asked him, "Don't you think it's getting too hot during the service?" Of course, at that moment he said yes, but the expression on his face had already changed. That was when I took my chance: "Pastor, don't you think it would be useful to have those big fans – just like the ones at the banks – here in the church?" He replied, "Of course! Do you want to donate some to the church?" I said right away, "Not donate, but I want to sell two of them to buy my bike!" He answered right away, "Does your mother know about that?" And I said, "Of course, she was the one who gave me the idea!" And he replied as he should, "I'll think about it and let you know."

It took a few weeks for him to give me an answer, but that didn't stop me from insisting on every single service. When I saw the sisters sweating, I looked at the pastor and pointed at them; and, of course, at the end of each service, I gently reminded him of the fact that it was very hot inside the church.

After a few weeks, he asked, "But how much is this bike?" I told him the price—obviously, at that point, I already knew everything I had to know about that bike. The pastor called my mom that same week and made the purchase. But there was a small detail – I would have to deliver the fans to the church. That was when I learned that it's not just about selling, you need to know how to plan some parts of the business such as, in this case, the delivery. I used all my strength to push those gigantic fans up the hill. But since I had been living in the same place for many years, and at that time, there were many carters, I quickly spotted one and asked for help. Fortunately, I was able to make the delivery and, with the money in my hand, I went to the store and bought my BMX.

The point I want to share with this story is that, as impossible as your dream may seem, there is always a fan in a dark room that you can use to start out. Perseverance is something you should always use to push you forward. Do not let things get you down when they seem too hard; after all, the highest places have less oxygen, and for this reason, there is always less competition. Think big, but start small, day after day, achievement after achievement, even if those things seem small. There is nothing better than the satisfaction of getting a task done, as little as it may seem today.

# Chapter 2

# PIGGY BANKS

When we were little, my father used to challenge us. He challenged us in many aspects of our lives. I remember when he taught me how to ride a motorbike when I was 13 years old, which is unthinkable nowadays. But it wasn't just that—he always talked about how computers would take over the world and how we had to prepare for it. However, there was one thing that really stuck with me. And it was the finances, valuable lessons we can learn with small things from our daily lives.

My father used to bring some cardboard piggy banks with metal frames (you've probably never seen one) and, every time he brought those, the challenge was: whoever filled it up first would get the same amount deposited in our savings, which means he would match the amount, and immediately get a profit of 100%. Unfortunately for me, I had a sister who was as eager as I was to save and find coins.

I wasn't always able to win the competition, but sometimes I did.

However, my father didn't deposit these coins in piggy banks; instead, he bought shares from the bank so that in the future we could take advantage of it. The truth is that I never found out what happened to those shares, but I think that, at some point, my father took this money and left us a small inheritance.

I am telling this story because I believe it is very important that we save money; we should always save. Not just when we have some money left at the end of the month – you need to save first and then live with what's left.

In life, we need to have priorities, and this is definitely one of the main ones because – as the subheading of my second book says – worse than not having money at the end of the month is not having it at the end of our lives. And for many people, this is an immutable truth, because once you're old, what magic thing can you do to get money? You don't have as much strength to work, and many times, your health and energy are gone; but also, our expenses are much higher than in the past, when we were young. One of the main reasons why I wrote this book is because, during my career as a financial planner, I heard a lot of people say, "If I had heard of this before, things would be different now!" Well, if you are reading this, there might still be time for you. So start saving in your piggy bank today. Many people say they don't have money, but is that true? Think about it; have you bought something this month? Have you bought a coffee, juice, a sandwich, something? Well, if the answer was yes, then you do have money, but it seems like you are neglecting it.

I remember when I released my first book, *Where does your money go?* This book was born from a radio show at Vinha FM, where I gave tips and spoke about personal financial planning. Many people talked to me, but I remember one young man who called to give his testimony. He told me he never saved money before in his life, but after listening to me on the radio, he had started to save. Soon, with that money, he was able to buy a calf and put it in his uncle's farm. The calf grew up and he sold it, and now he was buying two calves with the money he had saved plus the profit he got with the sale of the first one. Look how wonderful; this young man became a very successful person! You can think, *no way, it's just a calf...* But so what? He was able to double his assets in less than one year. Imagine if he does that for the next 20 years? Let's do the math. Take your calculator and multiply by two, 20 times. Start with the number 1 and multiply it. If you did this exercise, you might have repeated it a couple of times, thinking you did something wrong, but the reality is that you are correct – the final number is 1,048,576 (one million, forty-eight thousand, five hundred and seventy-six) calves!!

Of course, I'm not saying that he is going to double his funds every year, but the main idea is compound interests – this is the concept from which we can relate exponential equations, that is, the variations increase with the interval. In your case, the younger you are, the more you can accumulate, because the interests will do most of the work for you. Look at what Albert Einstein said about this: "Compound interest is the 8th wonder of the world. He who understands it earns it… He who doesn't, pays it".

My suggestion is that you start now. Don't just stand there – think of how you can save, fill your piggy bank and, in a very near future, your bank account.

# Chapter 3

# THE BLACK BOOK

Many things left a lasting impression on me during my childhood. I remember my mother sitting on the bed with my youngest sister, making the budget for the month. I didn't understand what they were doing in that room, in front of the old green safe, after all, there was nothing but paper in there. I think my mother didn't even lock that thing, so that in case a burglar came in the house, she wouldn't have a hard time opening it.

I always heard my mother talk about a black book, but what was so important about that book? Well, what they spent hours and hours doing, sitting on the bed with that book, was our budget. That's right; my mother planned the budget before the start of each month, and do you know why? Because otherwise, we wouldn't have enough money to get by. It was a hard time, but full of learning. I learned at a very young age to not spend more than I earned, and even with all the hard times we went through, we never had any debt.

At the time, we were five people in the house: my mother, my three sisters, and me. We lived in a big house in the corner, one of the largest houses in the neighborhood. However, we had to live with very little and make that little be enough. And that was possible because we planned. Before starting to earn her retirement, my mother already knew exactly how much she could spend and what to spend it with. This was in the late '80s, early '90s, and it was a time of huge inflation at a staggering 80% per month. But even though we had hardship, we never lacked anything.

You have no idea how important planning is in your finances. Having a budget is like having a compass in high sea, it makes a difference between your financial life and death. If you don't have a direction to follow, then any place will be welcome, and in your finances, not having a direction is disastrous.

You need to start planning today. Think of where you want to be 12 months from now and write it down; then 5 years from now and write it down. This is how you plan. Now, you will need to know if you are following your plans, and for that, you need a gauge, and your gauge is your black book, your budget. It is what will let you know where your money is going, and with it, you also decide what to do with your money, so that you are not just floating adrift, with no direction.

Start by writing everything down. Put it in an app or spreadsheet, whatever you want to use. At the end of the first week, check how much you've spent, and do that for an entire month. When the month is over, sit down and check what you're spending money with. In the end, ask yourself: is this really what I want? Do I have money in my pocket or do I keep just giving it to others? Do I buy things because I need them need or just because I want to impress others? You will see that many times, the things we buy are the least necessary ones. Start thinking about your desires and needs – those who only fulfill their desires run out of money to meet their needs.

You will only have an overview of what you are doing if you put my suggestion into practice. Notice that a company has many departments, but the one that the boss visits the most is the financial department, and do you know why? Because it is the heart of the company. So why does your personal life have to be different? Be thorough with your expenses; after all, they're the only ones you can control.

Once you know *what* you're spending with, now you can choose *how* to spend your money. Be careful when determining how you're spending your money. Think, *am I sowing or eating?* In other words, is this money going to come back and bring me more money, or is it going away and I'll never see it again? Make your resources work for you, after all, money doesn't take vacation, sick leaves, coffee breaks – and money never sleeps.

# Chapter 4

# FAMILY COOPERATION

One of the memories that are still fresh in my mind is Saturdays at my house. It was cleanup day; my sisters woke up early to tidy the house, and although I was the youngest one, I also had some chores. We had many dogs at the time, and one of them was very big, so I had to clean up the garage and their kennels. Everyone looked forward to that moment, not because we had to clean the house, obviously, but because after cleaning, we went to the Country Club, and it was the highlight of our week. But before going to the club, we had to do our house chores. I remember all of us running around to finish quickly, but when my father was home, he reminded us that the lazy man works twice – that is, if you don't do something right, you have to do it again. But that was an interesting form of mutual cooperation in our house.

During the week, we all helped in our own way; my sisters washed the dishes, I fed the dogs, and my mom cleaned up the house and cooked. Thank God we always had someone who did our laundry, since during the '80s in Brazil, washing machines were rare.

I often remember that my mom preached against waste, but only after I grew up I found out that whenever we had leftover rice, it was added to the next day's new rice, and we ate it all without noticing the difference.

So you might be wondering about what this has to do with you. Everything! You are part of a family gear, and what you learn at home, you will take with yourself to the street, to work, to your company, and even to your house when you have one. It is important that you learn at a young age that saving is smart and necessary. Save on the little things. In my house, I teach my children that I don't pay for the energy when they turn off the lights, and things like that.

Maybe you're not old enough to work, but you can still keep your family's resources in the house. How? By spending less, helping with the house chores by cleaning your room, turning off the lights when you leave a room, don't let the fruits and vegetables go to waste. Anyway, small actions can make a huge difference in the life of a family if everyone works together for that.

Imagine that your parents spend $3,000 a month and that, out of these $3,000, $350 are given to a cleaning lady. But if you do your part, and your siblings as well, you can dismiss the maid and, as a family, you just earned a $4,200 bonus at the end of the year! That is more than a month's wage that you can save up to buy a new house or car, or maybe even to go on a trip. The important thing right now is not to think of what you are going to spend, but how much you can save together.

If your parents save now, they can accumulate resources to pay for your university in the future, or if that's not the case, they can start accumulating for their retirement, and like that, they will enable you to accumulate for your retirement once you're older, instead of financially relying on you when they're older. This is called a virtuous cycle.

All of those who earned money in life did it through hard work and effort. Maybe while you're reading this, you are thinking of those who steal from our nation, such as crooked businessmen or politicians, but I have news for you – the Bible says, "Do not be deceived: God cannot be mocked. A man reaps what he sows." (Gl 6:7).

So what are you waiting for? Stop spending your parents' money on electricity or water bills and help them save, because if you are sowing prosperity, you will definitely reap 100 times more prosperity as a result. And here is something else: Those who spend everything they have will never have everything they want.

# Chapter 5

# DIFFERENT JARS

I really enjoy saying that we should have different jars, or reserves, for different moments in life. I think of the time that has gone by, if yesterday I knew what I know today, how different my attitudes and decisions would have been! Sadly, we can't turn back time, but a new time is born with each morning, enabling us to make new decisions, based on our acquired experiences.

I want to share with you something that recently happened to me. We have a company that remodels and sells houses in a low-income neighborhood in Memphis. In these last months, we renovated and sold many houses, and my intention is to give the opportunity for low-income people to buy their own houses. Here in the United States, there are many programs for those who are buying their first home, and the government helps those people with a subsidized amount of up to $15,000 in some cases. That's a good amount for buying your first house, don't you think? In this specific case, the house was sold for $62,000, so the buyers are getting an incentive that matches almost a quarter of the value of the property. Unbelievable.

The problem is that the people who lived in these neighborhoods did not have access to financial education and, most times, they get in financial trouble. One of the candidates to buy this house was a middle-aged couple who never owned a house, but they came to see the property in a Corvette. That's right, a very expensive sports car. Of course, it wasn't the latest model, but with a car like that, the expenses are high. The problem is that today we got the news that, although their credit is OK, and they don't have any debt, they were not approved because they did not have any savings.

How interesting – here in the United States, a good consumer is benefitted from a system that differentiates them from a bad consumer with a system called FICO, and that allows banks to talk to each other through credit-regulating agencies. What happened in this specific case was that, by analyzing the client's profile, the bank who was giving the loan chose to not take the risk, because as the banker himself said, "Old habits die hard." He was talking about the habit of spending everything you have, of not saving, and being at the mercy of an extra expense that won't let them pay their bills.

For this reason, sadly, this couple will keep buying expensive cars, but they don't have a place to rest *their* heads and call it their home, for now.

Notice that wrong decisions lead to these types of consequences. Have you imagined being more than 50 years old and not having a home? Owning a house is very important for a couple's emotional stability, especially to the ladies.

I believe this couple chose poorly on how to organize their financial life. Maybe they never heard of how to plan their budget, or just didn't care about it.

Back to the jars, I want to warn you that everything you do in your finances has consequences, both positive and negative. There is no neutrality in finances - you are either earning or losing, there is no such thing as a tie. I think we need to have three different jars of money for different moments in life.

The first jar is for the short-term; your salary, you need to save money every month. And there is only one way to make this happen, which is by spending less than what you earn and paying yourself first. You need to save! Your savings are the most important battle in a war; however, it is only the first one. It is like knowing how to do math; if you don't know how to sum and subtract, you won't learn how to multiply and divide. So have savings, and it can only happen if you spend less than what you're earning, so know where your money is going!

You are going to start your first jar with the money you save. This will take some time, but before you do anything, you should save at least 6 to 12 months' worth of what you spend; that's right, not of what you earn, but what you spend. So, if you earn $1,000 and you spend $800, then you should first accumulate $4,800. This is your second jar, and once you have your $4,800, your goal now is not to spend it, but to multiply it so that it can quickly get to $9,600, which is 12 months' worth of expenses. Imagine being able to stop working for an entire year without having to change anything about your life? Now, imagine doing that when you're 55 years old and never having to work for money again! I know many people today who work because they love what they do, not because of money, and you know what? They earn much more now than they've ever earned before.

This reserve can pay for many things in your life, and even help you earn more. Imagine that in times of crisis, many things are sold at a very cheap price, but only those who have the money can buy it. These values can quickly multiply in your hands if you are careful and diligent.

Once you reached these amounts, treat yourself. Eat at a nice restaurant, buy a new shirt or dress. Give yourself the luxury to satisfy your desires, but not with your reserve, but with the new money you saved. The money you accumulate is not meant to be used for consumption yet.

Let's go now to the third jar, which for me, is the most important one, because this is the money that will take care of you when you can no longer work. Usually, this is a very large sum and you have to start saving as soon as possible. Remember I already mentioned compound interests, and among the many allies you need to have, interests are the most important ones. It is necessary that you save from an early age, even small amounts, but never even touch on what you've accumulated. Even if you go through situations of extreme necessity, live your life as if you didn't have this money because if you don't, the chances of you spending it are huge, and probably, you won't have this resource in the future.

The math here is not that simple, since we have to take into account the inflation, future interest rates, opportunity costs, and many other complicated things. There are countless books that can help you understand this, and it is not my intention to talk about these things. My role here is to get you thinking and motivated about saving for your future.

Think of your jars, are they emptier or fuller? On a daily basis, do you add or remove from your jar?

If I had a time machine and could travel to the future, how would I find you 30 or 40 years from now? Healthy, wealthy, and living a prosperous life? Or will I find you old, full of needs and disappointment? Make your life worth it, don't just invest in things that will give you money – it would be too shallow to live like this – but don't despise this asset that has its worth.

Be accountable for your attitudes and your future, the reins of your future are in your hands, and you are the one who chooses which path to follow. It's no use saying that the government is bad, or that the bank manager didn't help you get the loan for your house. It is your responsibility; you can't ride a Corvette if you still don't have an apartment or house to live in. Don't use your money in such a wrong way, your money has to work for you and not the other way around. It is as wiser people say, "Don't complain about things you allow to happen."

# Chapter 6

# HONESTY AND TRANSPARENCY

You know, I lived in my parent's house until my 20's, and I always heard my mother say that our reputation is like a bag of feathers: if you throw it up in the wind, you will never recover all the feathers.

This always made me imagine a bag full of feathers being thrown high towards the sky and coming back empty. I kept thinking to myself, *wow… it must be really hard to get all the feathers back.* As time went by, I grew to understand what she meant. During these 20 years I lived with my mom, we never had any collectors knocking at our door, I never heard of my mom having a bounced check, and I am sure things haven't changed until this day. She always cared for her reputation and was very transparent in her negotiations and intentions.

You don't build character overnight, it is like a wooden sculpture, it is a slow process. It took me 20 years next to her, listening to her every day, but – even more importantly – watching her attitudes, as little as they were. Even if nobody was watching, she always cared about what's true.

When I first moved to the United States, in 1994, I witnessed a country that lived Christian principles, and people believed in one another. I remember a company that sold CDs. The way it worked was that you paid a few cents of a dollar and you were quickly delivered 10 CDs of your choice. However, you committed to buying 10 more CDs at regular price for 10 months. In the gas stations, you filled up first, and then you paid for it. Things like that were normal, but unfortunately, some people started buying the CDs using fake names, getting them first and not respecting their part of the agreement. Other people left the gas stations without paying for the gas and, sadly, when I came back in 2015, a lot had changed in these 21 years.

But I still believe that a person's word is more valuable than a contract when that person has character.

Sadly, in the world that we live in today, you can't be so naive as to not write down what you're doing. It's scary how many people lie, and some of them get to the point of believing their lies. For this reason, as a lawyer once told me, if you are willing to do what you are saying, then there is no reason not to put it on paper.

I believe there are still people whose words are worth more than a bunch of contracts, but unfortunately, we have to live in a world that is lost in its own rules and sins.

But for you, who maybe haven't started your professional life, or if you are starting your career now, believe me, some employers dream of having someone who is trustworthy, they need someone they can trust to be next to them. Start slowly, showing you are not just someone else who wants to take advantage of them. Dream high, but start with your feet well planted on the ground.

When you get the opportunity to take the quickest way up, think twice. When you get the opportunity to bring down someone else so you can succeed, rethink your position. When you have the opportunity to earn a lot of money by harming others, check if it really is worth it.

Your name has a lot of worth, and it probably is one of the only thing you will take with you when it's time for you to leave this world. How do you want to be remembered? What is the legacy you are going to leave to your children?

I was once asked if my father left me any debt, if I would pay for them, and I said yes. I believe in that, I believe that our name is worth a lot and it speaks highly of us.

Sadly, in our adult lives, success comes hand in hand with the attacks. Many people are slandered and reproached, but remember that everything a man sows, he will reap. If you sow righteousness and honesty, you can rest assured that you will be acknowledged. The book of Proverbs 22:29

says this, "Do you see someone skilled in their work? They will serve before kings; they will not serve before officials of low rank."

Look at this quote, which in other versions says, "… if you do your job well…" – doing your job well is being honest, transparent, diligent, and the Bible says that – "… you shall stand before kings."

I want to stand among the kings of this land, how about you?

For this reason, I can't sell myself for "crumbs," as big as they are, even because if I don't stand among the kings of this land, one day I will meet the King of Kings.

Think about it and remember that the right thing is right, even if no one is doing it, and the wrong thing is wrong even if everyone else is doing it.

# Chapter 7

# ACCUMULATING WHAT YOU DON'T NEED AND RUNNING OUT OF WHAT YOU NEED

While I write this book, I keep thinking about the experiences in my past, but I can't discard what I have learned and seen in these last 3 years I have been living in the United States.

I bought a house at an auction, which was sold for less than half of its market price. It is a house that was built in the 70's, when construction companies gave a lot of importance to details and material quality. It is a house with a beautiful garden and trees that have been there for decades, and at some point in the past, it had a lot of glory and glamour. Imagine being in a 40-year-old house, with a central vacuuming system and lots of fantastic details.

When I won the auction, I knew the house was being inhabited, because I obviously researched the properties I wanted to buy. When I took possession of the house, the owner's belongings were still in there, and I had to go through a painful eviction process, requiring the help of public authority to do so.

When I went inside the house for the first time, I was staggered; I realized in how much of a mess the previous owner was living, and it didn't surprise me that he lost his house for not paying his mortgage. The large round wooden table was covered by mail, bills, and more bills. After the previous owner moved out, I found an electricity bill from 2001 that had never been opened – imagine that, a bill from 16 years ago that was untouched, without being given any importance.

But what drew my attention the most was the amount of trash that man had accumulated. He lived in a mess that I never thought could even exist. But, on the other hand, he had more than 6 TVs – and not old, obsolete TVs. I'm talking about a curved 60" TV from a famous brand, which I think must be worth a lot of money. And that wasn't everything – among his belongings, he had all types of clothes, tools, more than four washing machines and dryers, books that had never been opened, even CDs and magazines that were untouched. Now, I ask you: why so much paraphernalia?

This same person, at some point, gave in to the desire to have what he didn't need, getting into a crazy wave of consumerism, which led to the loss of an asset that truly had some value – his house!

Notice that there is much to learn with this: when we buy what we don't need and spend our money with unimportant things, sooner or later, we won't have money for necessary things. As the good old saying goes, *a fool and his money are easily parted.* For this and other reasons you, while you're young, should acquire good habits, and one of them is saving. Don't let your desires take over you, don't let yourself get taken over by the NOW, by the happiness of getting what you don't need with the money you don't have.

I am talking about buying consumer goods with credit cards. What are consumer goods? According to the dictionary, it is nothing more than *a merchandise which goal is to satisfy the consumption needs of an individual or family; it can be classified as a* **durable good** *(automobile, fridge),* **semi-durable good** *(clothes and shoes), and* **non-durable good** *(food): it is common that in times of crisis, consumers decrease their consumption of durable goods and prioritize goods such as food.*

What makes things more complicated are the semi-durable goods, those that are part of every teenager's desire: those $300 sneakers, or those pants from a high fashion brand, or so many other things that will leave you chained to debt. This will undermine your power to buy important things for your life and future success.

Ask yourself this simple question when you spend the money you worked so hard for: *Is what I am buying going to generate more money or steal my money?* This is a very simple thing but, unfortunately, many adults, doctors, engineers, lawyers, teachers, economists, and so many others who have high academic education levels can't hold back and say no to consumption. We are a generation that wants everything now! We get stressed out when we need to wait for a minute in front of the microwave to warm up some milk, we get annoyed when the internet takes a few extra seconds to provide us information that in the past, we had to read through many books to get. We are the generation of impatience, but look at what the Book of Wisdom has to teach us about patience: "Whoever is patient has great understanding, but one who is quick-tempered displays folly." (Pv 14.29 – NIV).

For this and other reasons, I invite you, who are reading this book, to think, analyze your life right now, and wonder where you want to be 20 years from now, and how you want to be 20 years from now? Do you want to be in debt or have your money working for you? That's right, money works day and night, it doesn't take vacation, it doesn't take a coffee break, it doesn't sue you – money never sleeps. But why am I saying that? How are you going to employ your money if you only have $10 left from your allowance, or if you can't even pay your bills by the end of the month?

My dear reader, no one starts running before learning how to walk, and before walking, we all crawl. Be like a baby and take your time, but also don't give up. Little by little you will learn how to save and make what you accumulated work for you. Haste makes waste. Thomas Edison, before making his first lamp work, admitted he had created 1000 wrong ways to build a lamp. Imagine if he had given up the first time? So don't rush into building your wealth, invest in yourself first, start small, but always think big. Remember that a marathon always starts with the first step, and those who start ahead don't always get first place.

# Chapter 8

# DON'T BE A FOOL

When I was young, I had the opportunity to work with an import-export company. When I went to my interview, I told the CEO that I wanted to learn a new craft. I was a 22-year-old young man with many dreams. I was living in Boston and working day and night, but I knew that if I didn't have a career, it was very likely that I was going to spend my entire life never living up to the potential I knew I was meant for.

I remember that, while in Boston, I worked three jobs and I was able to earn good money. It was 1996, and at that time, I took home almost $800 per week. Imagine that, in one year, I could earn almost $42,000. But when I moved to Florida, I earned $1,500 per month. That's right, I was earning about $18,000 a year, which was a terrible deal, money-wise. My friends at the time told me, "You are crazy! Florida is for old, wealthy retired Americans, it is not a place for immigrants to make a living. Boston is much better, and the wages are higher."

But still, deep within me, something moved me to look for a career. I wanted to have a career, to know how to do something that would allow me to grow. That was when I started working with importing and exporting. I remember two people who were very special to me. They were two siblings, and one of them would later become my best friend for many years, and even the best man at my wedding. These siblings really helped me and taught me many things: the sister taught me how to work on a computer (I confess that at the time I barely knew what a mouse was), and, imagine that, their company bought and sold computer equipment and accessories. With them, I learned how to buy products that, even though I didn't know what they were, I had to convey confidence to those to whom I was supplying them. So I started learning to speak confidently, and even without understanding everything, to keep calm and negotiate. After the first setbacks, I started enjoying the job. I remember everything was very intense and fast-paced; in the same week that we received the orders from Brazil, we would make the estimate, compare prices, choose the best deal, buy the products, and ship them, and it was like that from Monday through Friday. It was very intense, but I really enjoyed it. Sometimes I would go to the office in the middle of the night because I couldn't sleep, since my mind couldn't stop thinking about the next day.

That was when an opportunity showed up. One of my childhood friends, with whom I used to speak on the phone, told me he was taking part in a bidding for these devices called palmtops. They were the most modern gadgets at the time, and it was huge. That was when I had the idea to give him a quote on these devices, after all, this is exactly what I did every day. Well, the next day, I looked for the price, added the company's margin, and even added 10% extra just to be sure; surprisingly enough, the price I gave my friend was much better than what he had. In the end, he won the bid and I made my first sale. From that day onward, I was no longer in the purchase sector, I was now working with sales. Some months went by and my job was now to sell to existing clients and prospect new clients, and in a short time, we already had many small clients buying a reasonable amount of products.

That was when, for unexpected reasons, the company closed their doors. One day, my boss just called me to his office and gave me the news. *Well*, I thought, *I already know how to buy and I have the contact from the people who buy*, so I asked for his permission and got in touch with my best client. When I proposed to become his purchase office in Miami, he said, "Of course!" Now I had become a purchase office in Miami for that client.

This is when my entrepreneurship started in the United States. I was almost 23 years old, with many dreams and hungry to succeed. I thought that I would be a millionaire by the time I turned 30, and I wasn't that far off – in 6 months, I had already saved $50,000. One day, this client called me to let me know some changes happened.

This was the operation: his company in Brazil entered the bids for São Paulo universities; on my end, I was in charge of making the purchases for them. When they won the bid, they sent the resources (money) via letters of credit; as soon as I shipped the merchandise, the bank draft was approved by my bank and I received the full amount. Since the amount included the operation's profit, I would later send his share through wire transfer.

Everything was going well, we had sold a few dozens of servers for many renowned universities in the State of Sao Paulo, when one day, I got a phone call. It was one of my partners, who told me something had gone wrong. The letter of credit had been sent to the Brazilian company, and not my company in the United States. With that, they would receive the money and later send my share. So he asked me if I would have enough money for the purchase, since this time, the operation surpassed my credit limit with the supplier. Keep in mind that I shared all my contacts with these "partners." Our intention was to open a branch of their company in Miami and I would be their operation partner in the United States, increasing their revenue by thousands of dollars.

I had no experience in the business world, and worse, I had no mentors. So I accepted to make the purchase and not only use the credit I had, as well as ALL of the money I had accumulated throughout those months. So I bought the equipment, which was many state-of-the-art servers from a famous brand. It was a total of 12 servers, and the purchase cost more than $50,000. I was looking forward to making the sale since it would give me a higher than average profit, and because I was risking my own capital, the Brazilian "partners" promised to send a larger share for my company. We would usually share the profits by 70/30, but this time, it would be 50/50, because I would not only bring in the credit but also my capital.

To make a long and unpleasant story short, they never paid me back. I took a plane, of course, and knocked on their doors; I went to Goiania, my home town, got a car and drove to Sao Paulo. When I got there, one of the partners was very surprised to see me and asked me to wait for the second partner to arrive. I was only 23 years old and, believe me, I looked like I was 18. When the other partner arrived, they invited me into their office so that we could talk, and that was when the senior partner said, loud and clear, that he wasn't going to pay me back. He said something I am never going to forget: "Aigo, you are very young, you have your whole life ahead of you, and this will come to you as a learning experience. I am not paying you back and that's it."

I argued and argued, but it was useless. He finished the meeting by saying, "I won't pay you even if you shoot me."

How horrible! There I was, for the first time facing the person with whom I had a commercial relationship for almost a year, and I realized I didn't know him. I was a fool; I never tried to know more about him, I never looked up who he was, and worse, I trusted him.

Years later, I would go through a very similar situation in which the attorney of a person who I cared dearly about would say this: "If you were saying the truth, you won't have any problems putting it on paper!"

The truth is, fortunately or unfortunately, that I learned that my word has much more value than any paper, but I can't be a fool to think that everyone else acts the same way.

For this reason, my young reader, I want to leave you a great tip – NEVER, EVER do business by only trusting words, as much as you know the other party. As a friend once told me, "In business, sometimes the other person doesn't want to harm you, but they end up doing that, even unintentionally." That is why we have attorneys and contracts. When you do any business, put everything on paper, black on white, sign it, and make the other person sign it too.

Sadly, that man was right – I learned the lesson. It was a bitter one, but I learned it.

Don't be a fool, business is business; friendship is friendship; brotherhood is brotherhood; don't get things mixed up.

# Chapter 9

# WHAT IS MONEY FOR?

There were only two days left for New Year's Eve 2018, and once again, the year had gone by very fast. In that Christmas, just like almost all others, my house was full. I hosted the family of a pastor  and their children and spouses, as well as a couple who lives here in Lakeland – TN.

We don't have family nearby, the closest one is 1,000 miles away, and the family we have is the favor of God for us, who sent us friends who are closer than brothers, a true gift from Heaven.

Our party was full of gifts, not necessarily the most expensive ones that money can buy, but this Christmas, the tree was full of gifts, which the children loved. My youngest daughter sometimes opened some of the wrappings, moved by her curiosity and anxiety.

But the true gift we received this Christmas was the memory that God became man, he lived among us and died for us. But who knows, maybe I will have other opportunities to write about this, but for now, I want to focus on the financial part, which, fortunately, is the area God has used me for.

The fact is that money can be good for many things; it can be clothes, it can be food, it can be health, but it could be drugs, prostitution, corruption, and/or a cause of sadness and a big mess. In reality, for a very long time, I thought money didn't have power, itself, to be anything until you gave it this power. But today my understanding is quite different. Money does have power, and the Bible treats it as a god, mammon, which competes with God Himself. But if you rule it and put it in the position of a servant, you can employ it well, and with that, you will reap the fruits of this good job. In other words, be diligent with him and treat him as a servant, not a lord in your life. It is necessary to understand that money does have power, it has the power to change your life for good, and many times, for bad.

But in this first case, I need you to pay attention to the fact that you can multiply it and every day have more, and with the "fruits," take advantage of what it can become, helping others and yourself. But if you always want to have it, never eat seeds, give time. Money, like everything in life, needs time to grow, remember that. This is one of the most important things when the subject is becoming rich: give money time to yield, and don't spend it on just anything.

54

In the case above, in which I mentioned Christmas in my house, it was employed in almost all scenarios, the only one in which it wasn't employed was love, which we express to each other through hugs, affection, words, and willingness to serve.

But the trip these friends made to my house cost the car, the gas, the time they didn't work, staying in my house, of course, the "housing costs," which in this case, has to be paid by someone, as well as the Christmas dinner, and so on. I think you get my point by now.

The reality is that we all know how to spend money, that is one of the easiest things in the world, but how about managing it? Can you, young reader, bear the pressure of having money? Or, in most cases, of not having it?

I want to reflect on a quote I heard from Neymar Jr., a famous soccer player, in a press conference: "If you were 24 years old and earned as much as I did, how would you behave?" (I am not in favor of his behavior, but he certainly has a point). Of course, he was justifying a kind of behavior which is obviously not the case here. The case here is the pressure that money puts on people. In his case, much more than most of us, mere mortals, will ever get to experience.

The point is that if you don't know how to deal with your money, it will have a lot of pressure in your life. With regards to having money or not, believe me, the pressure will be equally suffocating. In reality, the pressure of having it is many times much stronger than not having. And I am saying this from my own experience; I was talking about it with my wife not long ago. When I had to make payments that compromised my budget, I would be concerned as to how I would pay these bills. When I started having extra money, my concern was what I should do with it. After investing, many times, I felt a huge pressure of not saving enough. When I started saving appropriately, considering my income, my concern was with regard to my peers; I didn't earn enough to live like them. That is, I would never have peace of mind if I had remained in this group of friends, running around like lab rats, going nowhere. Only dissatisfaction would be waiting for me at the end of my life, like many others who only want to have for having, and don't know exactly the purpose of this wealth. The truth is that the secret is in a very simple word and can be very little used by our generation: contentment. I will dedicate an entire chapter to this later on in the book.

Young reader, I want to tell you that if you bought this book, you are interested in having a healthier financial life and maybe even get rich, but I want you to first ponder: why do you wish to have money? What will you do when you get there? What will you give up to get this wealth you long for?

On I Timothy 6:10, the Bible warns us: "For the **love of money** is a root of all kinds of evil. Some people, eager for money, **have wandered from the faith and pierced themselves with many griefs.**" *(highlighted by the author)*.

It is interesting to see that many people, out of love for money, have diverted from faith and tormented themselves.

A life of torment is what many people live if they don't understand the money they have. Many people are left without friends, family, or anyone. I don't want to give the impression that I despise money and what it can do for you - of course not. But I am saying it from my own experience – if it is not your servant and you don't have that very clear, it will become your lord, in a very subtle and unnoticeable way.

I was talking to my wife this morning, and while I worked in my home office, I smelled that chicken pie that only she knows how to make, and I thought about how blessed I am. So the Holy Spirit spoke to my heart that He will never leave me without bread and clothes. Look at what I Timothy 6:8 says, "But if we have food and clothing, we will be content with that." Notice how the word content appears once again.

Look, young reader, I don't want you to think that getting rich is a bad thing. But getting rich only to have money is terrible – you need to find a purpose for that. For many people, the truth is that they will never be millionaires. However, the promise of God is great: never, ever something will be missing, bread or clothes; you won't starve or be naked, which in this case, it means shame. The Lord will never leave you and, if you trust Him, you will never be ashamed.

Being rich is subjective. I don't consider myself to be rich. The reality is that, for many people who met me in the past, I went crazy when I moved to the United States. I no longer drive a Jaguar, I don't have a huge house in the gated community and I no longer boast many pens or watches. My trips are modest, it has been almost two years since I've been to Europe, where I used to go at least a couple of times a year. However, ask me if I'm happier or if my children know me better? If my wife spends more time with me, and me with her? If I have more time to get to know God? The answer is YES. My trips are now much more modest, but they still exist. My house is not as big, but it offers us plenty of comfort. My clothes aren't the same and I don't value the dress shirts, expensive watches, or renowned pens so much anymore; this is something that I left behind. Today I am concerned about something else, but know that even with all the change, money is still necessary, very necessary. However, it is no longer a lord in my life, my schedules, my friendships or my relationships. Today I feel free, stronger, with God. I think all of this experience I'm having is enabled by my Eternal Father, who saw something was out of place. I think the fact of adding this to the book is a mission. For those who want to be successful, God is success; having a simple life, without boasting. Believe me, not even Solomon, in all his glory, dressed like the wildflowers.

"Consider how the wildflowers grow. They do not labor or spin. Yet I tell you, not even Solomon in all his splendor was dressed like one of these." (Lucas 12:27)

I say that because the great trap of the devil with regards to money is taking away your peace of mind. If you have little or lots, he will always try to take away your peace, and Jesus himself warned us about it in the book of Lucas 12:28-31:

> *If that is how God clothes the grass of the field, which is here today, and tomorrow is thrown into the fire, how much more will he clothe you—you of little faith! And do not set your heart on what you will eat or drink; do not worry about it. For the pagan world runs after all such things, and your Father knows that you need them. But seek his kingdom, and these things will be given to you as well.*

For this reason, young reader, think well, pray a lot, and ask God in Heaven to be your financial advisor. Talk to Him about the subject, ask Him what He wants you to do with your resources and always save. Even if you don't know what to do with your money yet, save. Don't let it slip out of your hands. Always save it because, at the right time, I am sure you will understand the purpose of all these things, and remember the Parable of the Talents (Matthew 25:14). Just like that lord returned for his talents, our Lord will be at the door to check what you did with what was given to you, financially and spiritually. Rest assured that money is an excellent servant, but a terrible lord. So, as little as the savings is, whatever you are going to do, start now – don't wait until later, because the promise is that by being faithful with little, He will give you much. Having little or much, be content and grateful.

# Chapter 10

# ENJOY LIFE

After I turned 40, a lot of things changed in my worldview. One of them is that I couldn't do what I truly wanted to do, and instead, I had to do what life had imposed on me. I want to talk about the impositions of having a "SUCCESSFUL" life.

All of us, one way or another, seek acknowledgment, and this acknowledgment usually comes first from our parents, relationships, friendships, and then from our bosses or employees, and so on. But how much does it cost? How much does success cost to someone? I see many people buying what they don't need, with money they don't have, to impress people they don't know. This happens every day. Look around you, or maybe even look in the mirror, doesn't this happen in almost all social classes? Some people buy cars and mansions, go on expensive and fancy trips; others buy the latest smartphones or even expensive jeans, but these two profiles have something in common – many people buy with the money they still don't have, others spend everything they have, and in both cases, you are definitely set to disaster. Although it is dangerous because you are spending everything you have, there is still a third profile, which is those who have it and can spend it, but do it for the same reasons as those who can't – they want people's acknowledgment, also known as "showing off."

I'm not saying you can't do that, do whatever you want with your money, after all, it is yours – but don't complain about the results later.

The matter here is that even those who have a lot of money and like to show it, they are using it in the wrong way, and attracting people and situations to themselves that in the future will make them understand it wasn't worth it.

I have been learning, in these last years, that we don't need much to be happy. For example, you can go fishing on a $150,000 yacht or on a $1,000 boat. After all, the river in which you fish is the same, and maybe the equipment will give you more comfort, but at what cost? And if you do it to get other people's attention, that can be extremely dangerous, not only safety-wise but also in the sense of the type of people you will attract. This is the reason why many people don't have true friends, because they know this is true and many "friends" choose wealth over people, so they isolate themselves in their mansions because they think everyone wants to take advantage of what they have.

So my question here is, why? Why have all this money if you won't have someone with whom you can enjoy it? This new age of technology brings with it a surprising void; it makes us extremely connected, but scarily isolated. Everyone shares how happy they are on social media, with their smiling families doing amazing things, but then I ask you, at what cost? Why can't I sit on my house's porch just to watch life passing by, the birds singing, and kids playing? I wonder if when God created us, he thought we would have to be connected 24/7 to a screen? Or did He think we would be doing amazing things all the time? The problem with our generation is that we don't want to be bored; we run away from frustration and seek immediate pleasure.

For this reason, when I suggest you enjoy life, I mean that you do it FREELY, not caring about appearances, what others will think of you – just allow yourself to live!

A few days ago I went to a spring festival in my city. We live in a town with 14,000 people in a county with 1,300,000 inhabitants. People started arriving and putting their chairs in front of the stage, and just slowly getting themselves comfortable. I watched the children running, the food trucks selling food, the trampoline was set up, and do you know what happened when the music started? Nothing! That's right, most people just remained seated, scared of exposing themselves. Even those who were with us didn't want to dance and have fun.

Oops, did I say dance? You must have thought, "But isn't he a Christian?" Yes, I am a Christian, and I am a member of a Baptist Church. Does that mean I'm a Baptist and I dance? Yes, the truth is I'm neither from Paul or Apollo, I am from the Lord Jesus Christ of Nazareth, who came to the world so that I could live a life of abundance, but abundance of what? Abundance of freedom, because He came to free those in captivity and oppressed, He came to free me from the trends, of those things Salomon calls vanity. Yes, vanity. A lot of things we do is out of vanity, and a lot of things we don't do is to preserve our "image," but you know what? When you are sure that you are a son of God and you know you are loved, all of it stays behind. I can be free without being libertine; I can be free without scandalizing my brother; I can be free and still provide good testimony; I can be free and live as God created me, to be captive of His love! I don't need to shock anyone with my freedom, but I also don't need to deprive myself of things because of others. What God wants from us is common sense and balance. We need to have a balanced life.

So when I suggest you enjoy life, take advantage of it, have time to share good moments with those you love: go for a walk, talk to your wife and kids, take care of your house, clean up your garage, mow the lawn, bathe your dog instead of taking it to the pet store, wash your car. Do simple things and live simply. If you are too young and you still don't have these things, then help your parents at home and do your house chores. Call your brother and ask him if he needs anything. Talk to people, make friends. If you don't know anyone, then introduce yourself. If you have been living in a neighborhood for more than a year

64

and you don't know your neighbor, bake a cake, take it to their house, and introduce your family. Stop thinking of what people will say and think of you, don't be a fool. We only have one life and it goes by too fast, and for this reason, young reader, I tell you to enjoy your life with long-lasting things. Your relationships will be long-lasting if you invest in them, invest in people, make friends, build relationships with people who want and seek the same as you. Run away from those who want to take more than laughter and friendship from you and be careful with those who are luring you into their "armies." Pay attention to the vanities of life and the "success" some claim to know – success is relative. When I used to work with foreign trade, my boss and I were at a fair in Mexico and he, who owned the company, confided me with something that struck a nerve on me: "My wife loves going to Paris, she goes there almost every month. But I hate it, what I really love is to go fishing in Araguaia[1]" If, for you, success is earning 1 billion dollars, then go ahead. But if it is to be a missionary in India and live as they do, go ahead. Just remember that whatever your decision is, that you are doing it out of personal conviction and that you and your family will pay the price for it.

---

1. The Araguaia River (Portuguese: Rio Araguaia) is one of the major rivers of Brazil, though it is almost equal in volume at its confluence with the Tocantins. It has a total length of approximately 2,627 km. Araguaia means "river of (red) macaws" in the Tupi language.

# Chapter 11

# DREAMS AND QUALIFICATION

I only remember a few things from my childhood. I recently learned this usually happens with hyperactive people. I don't know whether that really is true, but I have few recollections from my childhood.

But with regards to my qualification, I remember my father saying, "Son, computers are going to take over the world." The year was 1988 and at that time, few places offered computer course, and I confess that I never liked programming. However, to work on a bank, I had to take a typing course, which was long, and we spent long hours typing many letters and texts on a sheet of paper. Ask your parents what "a s d f g" means, and they maybe could explain it to you.

But, back to the point, when I was 13, I took the typing course, because as my mother always said, "Those who don't use their heads make their bodies suffer." Every day, after school, volleyball, and swimming practice, I used to walk to my typing lessons, from Monday to Friday, and I did that for many months. I used to complain a lot because I was always tired, but my mother, with the wisdom of an outstanding psychologist, told me, "You either go, or I will hit you in the back with a broomstick." Well, you don't need to be a genius to know that I always made it to class, and in the end, I graduated. I still have my diploma to prove it.

Again, it wasn't easy, and it was not enjoyable at all, but it was necessary, even though I didn't understand why, but I believed on what my mother and father said, and for them, having a typing certificate was like having a high school diploma, it was a key step to getting somewhere in life. Well, the years went by and I was 16 years old, I could finally start working and, since my father worked for the Bradesco Bank for almost 40 years, now it was my turn to join the Bank.

I started as a clerk, and after a few days, I was sent to Goiania to take a telex[2] operator course. After working with telex for a while, I earned a new role, and I was in charge of the checkbook and bounced checks department. But I was still working with telex, so I had different roles in

______________

2. Telex is an international written communication system which prevailed until the end of the 20th century. It consisted of a global network with a numeric address plan, with unique terminals that could send written messages to any other terminal. It still works in many countries, although the number of subscribers is dropping after the creation of the email, which is cheaper. The terminals looked and worked like typewriters that were connected to a telephone-like network. Available on: https://pt.wikipedia.org/wiki/Telex Accessed on Sep 27th, 2018.

the bank. But everything in that place was exciting; I loved working there. However, many times in the morning, I had a hard time waking up because I studied at night and worked during the day. My mother, with much love and many broomsticks, was always there in the mornings to give me encouragement and reasons to get up. What I want to make clear is that during this time at the bank, I had to be prepared, take many courses, and when I turned 19, I left the company due to payroll cutbacks. The choice was down to me, a single young man, or another employee, who was married and had a newborn daughter. I think the bank made the right choice and fired me.

My cousin Jaci Gere, at the time, came from the United States to visit us. I remember as if it were today that when the phone rang, I was reading Lair Ribeiro's book, *O sucesso não ocorre por acaso* ("Success doesn't happen by chance"), preparing myself, and looking for something else. When my cousin visited us, she invited me to spend some time in the United States. I accepted her invitation and ended up moving to Seattle.

Notice that there is a great lesson here, and maybe my life would be completely different. I went to live with my cousin, her husband, and children. For three months, I lived with this amazing family, but I wasn't patient. They clearly welcomed me and wanted the best for me, they wanted me to study, and I lived in their home for some time, but I wanted to work, I wanted to live the American dream. So I quit my studies and moved to New York. That was a huge mistake – I delayed my studies in years, and I will never know the price I've paid for that. Who knows how different my life would have been if I had finished my university degree at that time.

You know, young reader, you only have now to live, tomorrow comes too fast, so don't waste time taking detours from your purposes. Be aware that there are seasons in life, and the season you're in right now is not meant to give fruits, or earn money, but to prepare yourself. Here in the United States, the salary for an executive in my town starts at around $60,000, but a senior executive earns as much as $180,000. If you have a blue-collar job, you will hardly be able to take such amounts home, unless you own your own business, which also doesn't happen overnight. Everything in life takes time to be achieved, and to reach a leading role you need to be good at what you do, and the more information you accumulate, the better. But don't be mistaken – you won't go anywhere just with information. You need to work hard, do what no one is willing to do (as long as it's legal and moral), give more of yourself, go beyond, think outside the box, and be willing to believe in yourself.

Nothing is easy at first, but after some time, and with the right tools, I am sure that success can be reached. Don't give up on your dreams, remember that Thomas Edison tried more than 1,000 times before he invented the lamp. See what he replied when someone suggested he should give up: "We have advanced 1,000 steps towards the final success." Get qualified, because when the right moment comes, you will have the right tools to make your light enlighten many people, and maybe not just many people, but humanity as a whole. That was Thomas Edison's legacy, have you thought about what could be yours?

# Chapter 12

# FEARLESS

You know that every father is proud of their children, and I could not be any different. When we moved to Lakeland, before buying a house, I wanted to get to know the city and my neighborhood, and for this reason, we rented a house for a year. I loved living in that place, I lived on El Hill street. It was a really nice house, with large rooms, and a very comfortable living room – nothing too fancy, but our family had a lot of fun in that place. As the name of the street suggests, our house was on top of a small hill, next to a golf course. When it snowed, we used to slide down the hill.

We moved to that house in 2017. My oldest daughter was 12, my son was 10, and my youngest daughter was only 8 years old. I always encouraged my children to have their own money, I want them to learn how to master it instead of being mastered by it. I think if you don't establish your domain over your capital, it will certainly do that to you (I will talk a little bit about this later). When we moved to this new house, because it was bigger than the one we used to live in at Florida, my wife and I thought it was best to give the children some chores. Besides their regular chores, they could also earn some extra money to buy what they wanted, but when your father is a financial planner, your life won't be that easy. I always like to encourage my children to save, and this is what I suggested them to do: the one who finished the year with more money in their hands would have a bank account on their name, and I would deposit the same amount they saved.

With that, I started to see some competition among them, but not only that, I realized they were looking for alternatives to earn more money (thinking outside the box). When spring came, we started mowing the lawn of the house, and other services started to appear. However, one day, after we finished cleaning our backyard and we started its maintenance, my wife noticed there were many golf balls around the yard. She filled some jars, which in the end, became a bucket full of balls. The main task had been completed - now the challenge was to convert these balls into money.

I talked to my children and suggested they should sell these balls to the people who were passing by the golf course every day, but they were too embarrassed and, even worse, afraid of getting rejected. I tried talking to them many times, but nothing I told them would convince them. It was then, on a Sunday morning, before going to church, that I was looking out my living room window and I saw two men that were looking at our yard. They were certainly looking for their ball, but they could never jump our fence without our permission, even if they knew where it landed, which wasn't the case.

I saw the opportunity and spoke to my children, but none of them wanted to do it, until my youngest one, very bravely, said, "I'll do it, daddy." And when she got to the door, she turned to me and asked, "But what if they say no?" I said, "You already have a no, go get a yes and negotiate the price." I had already said that the bucket was worth around 10 bucks, and that they could sell it for this amount. She went down to those men and I was watching by the door – I greeted them, but made sure she went there alone. When she offered the bucket full of balls, one of them said, "I will give you 5 dollars for it," to which she replied, "No, no, I want 10." He tried to negotiate a few times and she always looked at me like, "What should I do, daddy?" I just looked at her, supporting her, but without saying a word. She negotiated with him, and in the end, she didn't just get the 10 dollars, but he also gave her a two-dollar tip.

Keep in mind that this is how things in life work: if you don't overcome your fears, your limitations, and you don't negotiate with the challenges that will appear, you will hardly get where you want. To succeed in life, you need to insist, overcome your fears, and dive into the opportunities. What happens is that, from a young age, you hear: "Don't do that because it's dangerous," "Don't think this because it won't work." And you start developing a limiting mindset, which makes you believe you've lost even before you tried. How many opportunities have you left behind simply because you didn't want to get exposed, afraid of embarrassing yourself?

How many discounts you didn't get because you were embarrassed of whoever was next to you, and because of that, you spent more money?

Stop letting the external environment dominate you, stop thinking you can't do it, and dive into the opportunities. Take more risks, live more, but do it moderately and make sure your Father will be there with you, as Moses said on Exodus 33.15: "Then Moses said to him, "If your Presence does not go with us, do not send us up from here."  When you need to make a decision to risk yourself, to dive into a project, before you do anything, look up, as my daughter did, to make sure that I was standing by the door. Do the same thing with your Heavenly Father, look up to where our aid comes from, and ask Him, "Father, are You coming with me? Because I don't want anything that isn't Yours in my life." Once you feel peace in your heart and decided to do it, just dive into it, and always negotiate, because remember that nothing is yours, everything is His, through Him, and for Him. So always do your best and don't be scared, because true love drives out all fears.

# Chapter 13

# GETTING TO KNOW YOUR HEART

You know that the Bible teaches us to guard our hearts and also to ask God to examine it. Why do you think the Bible talks about it? One of the reasons for that is on Proverbs verse 23: "Keep your heart with all vigilance, for from it flow the springs of life." Look how fascinating, we need to keep our hearts with all vigilance because from it flow the springs of life, which means we need to guard our hearts because life comes out of it. If a water spring is contaminated, the entire river will be contaminated. This means that if your heart is contaminated, everything you do will also be immediately contaminated.

I was raised by my mother and I have four sisters and a brother. I am the youngest one, and when my siblings started getting married, as I grew up, I watched them leave the house to start their own families. My mother, on the other hand, always treated me like the boy of the house. She always said that I was a man, but I never had much influence from my father because he was always out working and managing his business: the farms and the bank where he worked. So I didn't get much influence from my father in business, and with that, I never had any malice for things.

It so happens that when I started working at the bank when I was 16, I started noticing a different world than the one I knew at home. My mother always made sure we had a Christian education, based on the word as our greatest good. But in the business world, sadly, people don't act that way, and they always put business before the word or other people.

When I started to notice how the real world works, it was a shock, and I started to harden my heart to bear a lot of what happened, especially when I moved to the United States when I was 20 years old. I was still a boy with no experience, living by myself, and I went through many struggles, even hunger. Even though I lived near some Brazilians, the only reason why I wasn't completely helpless was that I had a roommate who brought me some slices of pizza and salad at night. This lasted a little over a week, and thank God, I found a job.

But every experience I lived at the time hardened my heart. What happens is that when I started working and prospering, I had some money that could bring me some security so that I never had to go through this type of situation again. I didn't know anything about trusting God to take care of me; when I was a child, my own father told me that I had to fend for myself, and that stuck with me. How could I trust God, who is my Father, if I could not count on my natural father, whom I could see and touch? I didn't believe that I could count on anyone to provide for myself. God was still about to perform some work in my life.

Time went by and I became rougher and rougher, both to myself and the people around me. I only spoke harsh words, and I often thought to myself, *life isn't hard with anyone, people are too soft.*

Notice, young reader, that this seems to have nothing to do with money, but my toughness grew as my financial independence increased. The more independent I became, the tougher I got, and do you know why? Because money brings us this illusion, it isn't as neutral as I imagined and wrote in my first book. The truth is that the Bible treats money like a god, which means that it isn't exactly what I wanted, and God had to bring me back to the United States to teach me that, even though I was 44 years old.

You know, life with God is an eternal learning process, and I am not ashamed to say that I am still learning and being shaped every day. However, although I can change, God's words are eternal and He teaches us to guard our hearts and also teaches us to allow Him to examine our hearts so that he can show what is within ourselves. Today I know that I have a Father with whom I can count at any moment, and that He never forsakes me. This is a difficult process for those who are older, but it doesn't have to be like this with you.

You can learn while you're still young how to deal with situations like these. If you bought this book, it means you are willing to change something in your life; if you really are willing to learn how to manage your resources and earn money, then also learn how to guard what will influence all areas in your life, which is your heart. Talk to God, ask Him to not allow money to become an idol in your life. Know that the Bible talks about money as something that cannot be seen as neutral, because it isn't. We cannot just take some verses out of context, we need to have a wide understanding of what the Bible says about it.

Many people compare money to a brick. A brick can break a window or an arm, but it can build hospitals and houses. I don't believe money is like a brick, after all, money is much more than an object: it is a reserve of value; it is an exchange system; it is the way for you to acquire countless things your heart desires. You can exchange money for houses, cars, boats, trips, power, fame, luxury, and status. Money can be a tool, but it can also be an idol.

The Bible describes money as something that seduces, suffocates, and captures us, which witnesses against us, besides being a spirit, a false god, with its own will to deceive and enslave us. Jesus calls money "unjust" in Lucas 16.11. Psalms and Proverbs make a contrast between trusting God and trusting money. They warn us about the wrong ways to acquire and use riches, they warn us about acquiring so much that we become arrogant and unsatisfied, forgetting about our need to seek God.

The Word warns us, on I Timothy 6.9, that "…Those who want to get rich fall into temptation and a trap and into many foolish and harmful desires that plunge people into ruin and destruction."  However, in the hand of pure-hearted and wise saints, money can be an extraordinary tool for the expansion of the Kingdom of God on earth. Pray to God and ask Him to guard your heart, analyze why you want this resource and how He wants you to use it. Don't underestimate the power of money, because if it is not mastered and subjugated, it can become a god in your life and destroy you. And I'm not the one who's saying that – the Word of God is, tame money and make it your servant and not your lord. Pray for God to give you the wisdom you need to be prosperous and have your heart guarded by Him.

One way of doing that is, instead of satisfying your heart's desires and grow in wealth, ask God to grow in generosity. Talk to your Heavenly Father and confess your sins and ambitions to Him, ask God to inquire your heart and show your real intention about having businesses and money. Once God has spoken to you, it is time to ask Him for more clarity, and for him to change your heart so that you are not just one more person tithing high amounts, but for Him to grant you the change to tithe a high percentage of what you earn.

I once heard the following from a man of God: "It is not what you give that makes you generous, but what you retain." What a great revelation! And it is on the Bible - Jesus himself witnessed a person who did that, and I am talking about the poor widow and her offering. She didn't ask God for more money to bless the Kingdom of God, she gave everything that she had. What was in her heart was revealed at that moment. I am sure that the Lord blessed her very much.

What is in your heart? Why do you want to have money? And, if you already have it, why do you want to have more? This is very important for you to move forward and keep a pure heart. Don't be fooled, if the spring is contaminated, everything else will also be contaminated. The Word of God says that God cannot be mocked; everything the man sows, he will reap.

There is only one way of sowing, which is through seeds. What are you sowing? Look at your actions, your ideas, your true motivations. I confess that during many years my math was, if the church needs 1,000,000 for whatever reason, it means God will give his saints 10,000,000, so I wanted to be part of those who donated. This is wrong, and although I should ask to be part of those who donate, I should not do it with the intention of retaining more and more for myself.

Care for your heart like your greatest treasure, because it is. The spring of life flows out of it, as the Lord says, and remember that a way to check someone's heart is through what comes out of their mouth, because the Word of God says that the mouth speaks what the heart is full of.

We are going to discuss a bit more, in the next chapter, about some ways you can guard your heart and not believe in the devil's traps to entangle your life. Don't work to earn more money, because remember, it is not yours. You are only someone to whom this resource was trusted; with little or much, it was God who put you where you are now.

# Chapter 14

# STEWARDSHIP

In the previous chapter, I talked about knowing your heart and looking for the reasons in God why you want to have money. In this chapter, I want to teach you how to deal with this resource and your role in this equation, which must be divine.

In the Parable of the Talents, there is something great, which is the reward. I think what every servant of God wants to hear the most at the end of their lives is, "You have been faithful with a few things; I will put you in charge of many things. Come and share your master's happiness!" (Mt 25.21).

But for that to happen, we need to understand our part, what we need to do. In this parable, there was a lord (we also have a Lord), who trusted each of his servants with a certain amount. That is, those talents or financial resources weren't theirs. You know, young reader, for a long time I thought that God had trusted me many things and that I owned myself and my money. As long as I was "faithful" to Him, returning the tithes and offerings, I would look good. The truth is that with Christ, things are different: He came to give us grace, but he raised the level of our attitudes in all aspects, including how we manage money. What you have is His, not yours; and not 10%, but 100%. And, if this is not just a nice religious speech for you, have you spoken to the Lord about what you are doing with His money? How have your prayers been? "God, bless me with this, that, and that other thing?" Do you make your conversation with God a walk in the "supermarket of blessings," and in the end, you leave the check on Jesus' tab?

I am not against asking God, after all, you do have to ask, but is it just for you or for the people you know? For whom are you interceding? For whom have you been praying and giving yourself? You know, money has the power to become a god in many people's lives; because of it, people cheat, lie, steal, and even kill. So are you going to tell me this is a truly neutral object? Even many saints, in the ambition of achieving more "for the Kingdom," got lost, as the Bible warns us on 1 Timothy 6.10: "For the love of money is a root of all kinds of evil. Some people, eager for money, have wandered from the faith and pierced themselves with many griefs." I don't know about you, but when I had the revelation that I could be one of these people that wander from faith and are pierced with many griefs, I was truly terrified.

You know that a life with too much wealth can and will corrupt your heart, never doubt that. I'm not saying there aren't exceptions, but unfortunately, most people become tougher and greedier. Do you know any millionaires who wash their own cars? Or that take care of their gardens, or that do the dishes after dinner? You can say, "But this has nothing to do with that, just because I have money, it doesn't mean I don't love God anymore." That is not what I mean - you can love God and be arrogant.

Have you noticed how many times you have seen a very successful person getting out of their comfort zone to help someone that can't give them anything in return? I am not just talking about sending money, I am talking about getting out of their comfort zone, getting out of their way to help a brother with less and who needs more. The reality is that there are many people among us, believers, who think the more money they have the more they can do for the kingdom, and that's a lie. They are wrong in thinking the money is theirs; the money belongs to God and they are only the Lord's steward. The word steward means an individual who manages other people's houses. That's right, an individual whose job is only managing other people's assets, not his.

So, youngster, if you want to be rich to do things for the Kingdom, think again. You don't need to be rich to be a steward, and God encourages us to live a life of giving. Have you wondered why you want to be rich or "financially independent"? Because we don't believe that God will be able to keep taking care of us even at an old age, when we can't work. That is why we want and need to accumulate. The problem is reaching a point in which we lose track of what we need and we can't tell when something is just a luxury.

If today you live in your parents' house, it is very likely that if you got a brand-new car, you would be very happy, right? And I will tell you that you would maybe be happy for two years, and then you would see it as an old, obsolete car, and you would probably want to trade it. Do you know why? Because we are dissatisfied. Many of us, Christians, have reached a point that we never even dreamt we would, and we are still seeking more.

I remember I had a consultant who had a lot of sales and earned a lot of money, but he wouldn't go home anymore. I also earned from his sales, but I saw something wrong in his life, and it was his "love for money." One day I asked him how his marriage was doing, and he said, "fine." But his wife talked to my wife and cried a lot, saying her husband didn't give her or her children any attention. You know that many people fool themselves when they say that one day, when they have this or that, they will stop, but that's not true. This person still earns a lot of money, he no longer works with me, but he is still traveling a lot, with no time for his family. The question is: how much is enough? Believe me, you can't answer this question naturally, you need God's Holy Spirit to know the right amount so that you don't lose your heart.

I am a child of divorced parents, and there are many divorces in my family. When I got married, I called my wife and, in our wedding night, we prayed to God and consecrated our marriage to Him, asking that these divorce bonds were broken in our lives, and that was almost 15 years ago. I am saying that because you must do the same thing with money. Pray to God and ask Him to answer the following question: "How much do I need to manage the wealth the Lord is trusting me with and that is His?"

You don't need to be rich to be happy. In fact, if wealth was a sign of happiness, suicide rates wouldn't be so high in first-world countries. What you need, is Romans 12.2: "Do not conform to the pattern of this world, but be transformed by the renewing of your mind. Then you will be able to test and approve what God's will is—his good, pleasing and perfect will."  This verse is amazing!

The first part, "Do not conform," do not accept the pattern of this world. What our generation tells you that you need is a lie. Second part: "but be transformed by the renewing of your mind" – seek the Word of God so that your  mind can be renewed, outside of earthly patterns, that say that the more the better; outside of the patterns of churches that reach prosperity with a spiritual bias, saying that you need to be rich to bless the work. Instead, pray to have Christ's mind in your life. And the third part: "Then you will be able to test and approve what God's will is – his good, pleasing, and perfect will." I want to experience the good, pleasing, and perfect will of my Lord.

Youngster, ask God to give you wisdom, because He gives you everything you ask, but ask for it according to His will, and His will is in the Bible. Learn how to pray the Word of God, it is powerful. The greatest asset we have in our spiritual equity are the promises of God for our lives. Do not wander from the Word of God in any direction, let the Lord be the guide so you don't stumble, and so that, on that special day, the Lord can tell you: "You have been faithful with a few things; I will put you in charge of many things. Come and share your master's happiness!"

# Chapter 15

# ENTREPRENEURSHIP

I want to talk to you about entrepreneurship. As you read at the beginning of this book, I had my first business experience when I was 10 years old. When I was still living in Anapolis, I had the opportunity to make some deals, buy and sell cars, bikes, and even trade a scooter for a dirt bike. When I moved to the United States, and after the purchasing office in Miami, I went to Brazil to collect the money which I never got, and on the way back, I went to Goiânia to cry my disappointments out in my mother's house.

I was crushed, I had just destroyed my first business, and thank God I didn't have any debt, but all my savings had gone down the drain. That was when one of my sisters invited me to eat *acai*. My question was: "Aca what?" I had no idea what it was. She took me to this really nice place in Goiania, where they had a climbing wall and they served this purple thing full of granola, honey, and other things on top. I liked its flavor and I watched all those beautiful people, with very fit bodies. That was when it hit me: *I live near Miami and I never heard of this fruit… hmmm, I'm going to take advantage of my trading knowledge and I'll take this fruit to the United States.*

I briefly researched about it and I noticed that the best products were in Para. I called my father and he helped me find the best possible place for importing: the name is Tome-Açu. I contacted a cooperative, and after a lot of struggle, I convinced them to sell me the fruit to be exported. The process took about six months, and the few savings I had could barely cover for my new business, but I didn't let that stop me. I called my former boss, Cesar Cunha, and pitched him the idea. I invited him to become my partner, he said no, but helped me with the website and gave me a few tips. The first time, I imported 50kg of the fruit. When the açaí arrived in Miami, my customs broker called me and said, "The FDA (US Food and Drug Administration) is asking me what this is." I said, "It's fruit." And she replied, "But they don't know it and we have to run some tests on them." At the time, it cost, if I'm not mistaken, 500 dollars per fruit. Wow, I could not afford that, and all my savings were invested in that 50 kg of fruit. I picked up the phone and called Cesar again. He didn't want to be my partner but loaned me 500 dollars.

They ran the tests and the shipment was cleared. This time I wasn't able to profit from the fruit, because I was selling each kilo of açaí for 9 dollars, and it was enough to pay for my first shipment, but not to pay Cesar back. At the time, I was working two jobs, but I didn't give up. That was when *Taste of the Amazon* came up. I was selling to Brazilian stores in my area, during my work breaks, but the volume was still very low.

Three months and about two importations later, I decided I was going to open a kiosk at the beach. There was a restaurant inside a hotel in Fort Lauderdale whose owner was Brazilian, and it was a restaurant by the beach, with the sea in its yard. At that beach, there was an empty kiosk, and I had the idea to rent it. I talked to the owner of the restaurant, who agreed to rent me the kiosk. At that point, I had paid Cesar back and had a few savings.

I started with the kiosk on the beach, but I had never prepared açaí in my life. I learned a few recipes, but nothing tasted like the one I had in Goiania. So one day, a man approached me and asked me in Portuguese, but with an American accent, "Do you sell acai?" And I said, "Of course!", and I made him some. But he threw it away and told me, "You don't know how to make it, let me teach you." Well, an American jiu-jitsu wrestler who had lived in Rio for a few years taught me how to make acai in a bowl. He bought all the acai I had in the kiosk to take home, paid for the one he threw on the trash, and even tipped me.

That was all I needed – I just needed five more guys like him and I was going to get rich! But things are never that easy, and that was just a start. I had to invest more - my blender didn't grind the ice properly and I could never prepare it quickly enough. What happened is that the American guy had gym buddies, and soon they started going to my kiosk. And the wrestlers brought along their girlfriends and friends, and with so many athletes – with bodies of athletes, needless to say, people started wondering what those people were eating at the kiosk.

The hotel also offered jet ski rentals and they had a sand volleyball court. At the time, some Brazilian newspapers started being distribuite in the area. I saved up some money, talked to the restaurant owners, and we promoted a sand volleyball championship in the hotel, and of course, with free fruit juices for the competitors (at that point, I was importing about 500kg of fruit per import, and I offered about 8 flavors, such as *cupuaçu*, passionfruit, guava, and other tropical fruits).

In short, at the end of 8 months, my kiosk boomed and the owner of the restaurant wanted to renegotiate our terms. That was when I thought, *I'm going back to do what I know, which was wholesale.* The owner of the restaurant offered me to keep 50% of the business, and I politely said it wasn't fair to him. It was his business, he just needed to hire an employee, and I would be happy to sell him the fruits. So the owner started buying acai for the kiosk, as well as offering it at the restaurant, and I went out to visit other restaurants and local businesses.

It was hard at first, but in less than 12 months, I was controlling the market (I was the only one), and I was importing the fruits in containers. They were 10-ton containers that I sold in Florida and eight other states. That was when a unique opportunity came up: one of my main local buyers didn't pay me for 15 days, which was unusual, and I went to speak with him. The name of the coffee shop was Brasliced, and the owner – a young and hard-working man, but with no experience with numbers – told me he wasn't able to stay on the black. After analyzing everything, I offered to buy part of his restaurant, provide the fruits, and forgive his debt, and he accepted it.

But I couldn't be in two places at once, and that was when I met a young man who was starting his own business distributing Brazilian cheese bread. He was a young man from Minas Gerais who asked me to be his distributor in Florida, and I accepted right away. The year was 1999, close to 2000, and I was living "the best days of my life." I worked hard, but I was earning very well.

Then came the idea to expand my business to the American audience. I knew nothing about it, even less about financial planning, marketing, and business plans. Remember I quit school? I was moved by my own intuition for business, and believe me, that is not enough. I hired an engineering company to make the restaurant, I spent a fortune with all the store equipment and design. It was supposed to cost me 60 thousand dollars, and in the end, it cost 180 thousand. It was supposed to take 90 days, it took 6 months to open! It was a true disaster, and I could never get the store up and running.

In 2001, I heard that my coffee shop partner kept cash inside the old oven we didn't use, and I was no longer able to manage so many businesses. I sold my part and moved to Brazil in 2002, with way less money than I once had.

There is only one reason why I am telling you all this, which is, you need to get qualified and have mentors to help you when things aren't doing well. You can't do everything by yourself, you are not and will never be Superman. To grow, you need other people, and never underestimate the value of higher education. The business world is not for amateurs, and if you really want to be successful in this world, you need to be prepared.

As for your mentors, don't choose those who seem to be something, those with the best cars or biggest houses; look for those who can really prove their knowledge. Also, don't get caught up on the diplomas on the wall. I met people with an excellent curriculum, but who couldn't handle the pressure. In the business world, you need to have the guts to get into places no one dared to be. Today, the acai business in the United States is a huge, maybe billion-dollar business, but at the time, I didn't have the structure to bear it, and I believe God had other plans for me.

I remember my arrogance, because I was only 20-something and successful, and I thought that by the time I turned 30, I would be a multimillionaire, with yachts and big houses in Florida. But do you know where I was at 30 years old? I was in Brazil, starting over with my life, with a beautiful wife and a newborn daughter. On September

2004, my daughter Maria Luiza was born and, believe me, I wouldn't trade anything for the opportunity of having her in my arms.

The ways of God are higher than ours, and His dreams are much greater than yours. Think twice before making decisions by yourself; ask God to open your eyes so you suffer less and you don't have to go through so much to learn the Father's lesson. Today, I'm a happy man for everything that happened to me, I am grateful to God for saving me of the world and myself. You don't need to rule the world, but you need God to rule your heart. After you give your heart to Him, you can rest assured that He will give you what you need – which is not always what you want, but He will certainly give you what you *need*.

# Chapter 16

# BELIEVE IN YOUR DREAMS

When I returned to Brazil, I went back to Goiania and met Ludmilla, my wife, in a Wednesday meeting at the Videira Church, of which I was a member. About one year and a half later, we got married. I was working in a factory that manufactured bathroom accessories. The company sold all over Brazil and wanted to start selling abroad. One day I received an invitation from a friend to go to a meeting in Sao Paulo with a British guy so that he could tell me about a financial planning business.

I thought it was nice, but I barely had money to provide for my family, and at that time, I had gone back to school and I was in the third year of my Business Administration course, focused on Foreign Trade. But my wife encouraged me to go and I went to hear what the British man had to say. I spent an entire weekend with him - we started on Friday and finished on Sunday. At that point, I was working in this factory and traveling around the world; I had gone to China as an importer, to Mexico as an exporter, and I had visited many South American countries and even Dubai, but I didn't have much savings, I didn't earn very well as a manager, but I had the status of someone who was doing very well with all these trips. When I finish my training, I returned to Goiania by bus, because I only had enough miles to buy a one-way airplane ticket.

I traveled all night thinking of what I had learned, and I saw my life pass by in a flash. What the British man said made me think at a short, medium, and long-term, I had never seen my reality that way. I was 30 years old and I thought I was doing well, but the truth is that I wasn't consciously doing anything for my future. I wanted to succeed and have things, but I didn't have a plan, I wasn't a strategist, I had never thought about the days that I wouldn't be able to work, and I definitely never thought that one day someone would have the burden of taking care of me. I spent many hours doing self-analysis and feeling much fear inside that bus.

When I told Ludmilla what happened, she told me, "This business is for you." And I thought, "Are you crazy?" There's no fixed wage and I barely have a 6-month emergency fund, and worst, our daughter wasn't even one year old. So this time it was different, and I prayed to see what God had stored for us. The person who introduced me to this business was interested in this partnership and he would also earn from it, that is why at the time he offered me cost-share assistance, which made a huge difference, and I am thankful to him until this day.

So I made the decision, we were sure that God was in this business, and I went for it. Seven months later, I hadn't closed a single deal, and my cost-share assistance was over. I was crushed, but I married a woman of God who didn't give up. She prayed and told the Lord, "Lord, You confirmed us, my husband goes to work every day, he works as he should, but we haven't reaped any fruits. So, God, I am only eating again the day you change our luck."

I confess I don't have the same faith. Three days later, I was sitting at a coffee shop in Goiania, completely discouraged, sad, frustrated, and feeling sorry for myself, when my phone rang. It was a doctor with whom I had talked a few months ago, and he said he would call me back. He said, "Aigo, do you still work with planning?" I was very tempted to say, "No, I am giving up today!" But I said, "Yes, doctor, I am. How may I help you?" He said, "Come to my office today because I want to close a deal with  you." I could barely stand up – I had made it, it was true, now I could say I had a client.

When I got there, I tried to hide my trembling hands; when I left there with a (huge) contract, I could barely believe it, and he even referred me to ten other friends. I went to my house and told my wife, "You can eat now, the Lord has blessed us!" We were saved, I had closed my first deal. After that day, I got many clients in a month, when the usual for an advisor is having four contracts per month, but God gave us much more than that!

The promises of God go through the test of time, but they never fail. They are our biggest asset, don't forget, his promises for us are much greater and better than our dreams. Summarizing this story that happened 14 years ago, as a company, we had more than 600 active clients. Today, I am not living in Brazil, but I help almost 400 families, and God has given me the honor to take care of these clients for 14 years. Many of them have become friends, others became brothers. So trust the Lord and believe that He will do everything else.

> *My son, do not forget my teaching, but keep my commands in your heart, for they will prolong your life many years and bring you peace and prosperity. Let love and faithfulness never leave you; bind them around your neck, write them on the tablet of your heart. Then you will win favor and a good name in the sight of God and man.*
>
> *Trust in the Lord with all your heart and lean not on your own understanding; in all your ways submit to him, and he will make your paths straight. Do not be wise in your own eyes; fear the Lord and shun evil. This will bring health to your body and nourishment to your bones. Honor the Lord with your wealth, with the firstfruits of all your crops; then your barns will be filled to overflowing, and your vats will brim over with new wine.*

*My son, do not despise the Lord's discipline, and do not resent his rebuke, because the Lord disciplines those he loves, as a father the son he delights in. Blessed are those who find wisdom, those who gain understanding, for she is more profitable than silver and yields better returns than gold. She is more precious than rubies; nothing you desire can compare with her. Long life is in her right hand; in her left hand are riches and honor. Her ways are pleasant ways, and all her paths are peace. (Proverbs 3.1-17)*

# Chapter 17

# ALWAYS BELIEVE IN GOD

When I arrived in Brazil, I was quickly reinserted into the marketplace. However, I was no longer a business owner, but God is so good that I started as an executive in a company which owner knew me and my reputation. Sometime later, due to a belief disagreement, I left the company and lost my job.

That was right after my reunion with God. It was 2002 and I was 28 years old. It was a moment that I was going through a fresh start, it had been two months that I was back to living in my mother's house, and I was going to the Videira Church. At the time, there was only one building at the Setor Bueno District, and I was truly in love with Jesus. That was when, after a few months, I met a girl on a Wednesday at a life group meeting, and her name was Ludmilla. It was love at first sight, but I followed the advice from my brother-in-law and pastor, José Maurício, and focused only on one relationship: my relationship with Christ.

After a few months, my feelings for her only grew, and that was when I decided to open my heart to her. Unfortunately, she didn't feel the same way and I had to fight for her heart, but this is another long story that took about 6 months.

What happens is that during that time, I went back to school, I was accepted at the Business Administration school, I had to start over, but now I can say that it was worth it. These were difficult days, but now that I am more mature, I remember this time with much love.

It was a time with no money but with great friendships, such as my friend Aguinaldo Caixeta, who always encouraged me in my life with God, as well as my pastors, leaders, and so many people who were an important part of my life. If I can give you one piece of advice, youngster, is that you surround yourself with people who love God and try to find out the true purpose for which you were created. This will help you to not waste your precious time, and time is not only minutes or hours, but it is also life – remember that.

But back to Ludmilla, I wanted to start going out with her, but I didn't have a dollar in my pocket, I couldn't even afford school. At the time, my mother and my sister Edy, who lived in the United States, were the ones who helped me with my studies. And one day I got a call from a recruiting company from Goiania, to which I had sent my resume.

They invited me to try out for a foreign trade assistant job, and I thought to myself, *with my experience, I could at least start as a manager*, but I needed the job. So I went to the interview and, to my surprise, I wasn't hired.

I was frustrated and even upset about that situation. At that time I was dating Ludmilla and wanted to ask her to marry me, but how could I do that if I didn't even have a job? That was when, one morning, I was studying in my university's library, and my phone rang. It was the recruiting agency again, but this time, the position was for foreign trade manager, both for importing and exporting. There was my chance – I ran home, shaved, put on a suit and tie, and went to the interview.

At the time, I was willing to earn R$500 per month, I didn't care about the wage, what I wanted was an opportunity. I was interviewed by the owner of the company, and later I heard that it doesn't happen often. He asked me many questions and, in the end, he said, "But you know that the salary we are offering is 1,500 reals, right?" When he told me that, he looked down. I hadn't taken any neurolinguistics courses yet. But the Holy Spirit of God is in me wherever I go, and I felt it in my spirit that he was ashamed of offering me that amount. That was when I told him, "Mr. Gilberto, it's fine, I am willing to start with little and prove my worth." At the end of the day, I got hired, and I would get to see Europe, Asia, the Middle East, and other Latin American countries, representing that company.

Do you know what was the first thing I thought when I left that room? That now I could marry the love of my life.

The reality is that many times, your opportunity will come disguised as obstacles, or even as bad news, such as not getting hired for the job you wanted.

Many times, God needs to take things away from us to give us what He wants. We need to trust God because He always has the best for us.

I had to leave the United States, go back to Brazil, meet my wife, start my family, and only later, God brought me back to this land. But I am sure that this is not the end of my story, and that He has many other adventures for me.

God needs to be your biggest relationship, the center of your life, and you need to deposit your trust in him. The world tells you that you need to achieve things to be happy, that you need to be "successful" to be acknowledged. And I tell you this, young reader, that the world doesn't know what is written in Romans 12.2: "Do not conform to the pattern of this world, but be transformed by the renewing of your mind. Then you will be able to test and approve what God's will is—his good, pleasing and perfect will." There is a condition for you to experience the will of God in your life – you need to be out of the world's pattern, you need transformation, and this transformation comes from what you believe in, from your mind. You and I need the mind of Christ in us, we need to dive in the Word of God every day to have our minds transformed, and like that, we are going to prove His will for our lives, and believe me, it is much greater and better than ours.

I never believed I would have a wife and kids, I always had relationships with women who had been married and already had children. God gave me my own children. I never thought I could have a company, that I would employ people, and that I would be successful, but God also changed that. I never thought I would write a book, and even better, that someone would pay to read it and, once again, God changed that.

You know, our generation doesn't need rich young people, who can do many things for the Kingdom of God with the money they will earn from their jobs. What our generation needs are young people who are servants and obey their callings, who dedicate themselves and don't conform to the reality of this world. What our generation needs aren't princes, but "pierced ear slaves", young people who want to serve their Lord in a free and unobstructed way, not doing their own will, but dying to selves every day, while they walk towards Christ.

You can rest assured that He wants you as you are, but He won't let you remain the same because I am sure that He will take what you have to give you what He wants.

# Chapter 18

# CONTENTMENT

The dictionary described "contentment" as "a state of happiness and satisfaction." I remember my sweet mother saying after lunch: "You're not full, you're satisfied." Do you know what it is to be satisfied? In my case, in the example above, it was not having any more room in my stomach. I was satisfied.

You know that life is about being satisfied, being happy with what we have!

Probably, when you bought this book about finances, you must have thought that I was going to talk about 10 ways to earn more money, or even how to get out of debt in 12 days, or any other miraculous formula to quickly turn you into an expert in finances. But the reality is different - for you to be an expert in finances and have more money in your account, you just need to be content with what you already have!

You may think, but if I'm not ambitious, I won't get anywhere in life; if I settle, I won't go far, I will always be in the same place. Look, the word settled means conforming. I am not suggesting you are conformed, but I am saying that you need to be content. Content and grateful, and this will lead you into a state of happiness with what you have, and it will calm your heart for those things you desire.

Do you know what is a sales person's main goal? Making you wish for what they want to sell. Have you thought about it? It's very simple – think of that object you want to buy, the car you want to have someday; you will realize that you will get caught up on that, and you will constantly see that car or object every day. Ask someone you know who has a pregnant wife, they will say that it seems like every woman in the world is pregnant. It is very common that, during that time, their eyes are more focused on pregnant women, because their desire is to be a father and have a child in their arms, and for this reason, they start noticing pregnant women. This happens because your attention is focused on what you desire, but if you are content with what you have, you will certainly be much less propense to buy out of impulse.

Not just with buying, but this also happens with everything in life. Did you know that 100% of the times someone cheats on their partner, it happens because the couple lost interest in each other, and not because they are no longer happy with the other person? Speak to God and seek your contentment in Him. It is important that you understand that true success is being contented with yourself and your achievements.

I remember something that happened in Goiania, when a man sold his company for millions of dollars to a foreign group, and months later, this same person jumped off the balcony in his apartment. Money doesn't bring happiness, believe me, many millionaires are miserable. Money doesn't bring any type of happiness, the toys that you can buy with money will only entertain you for a while; the trips, luxury hotels, cars, boats, planes, it is all very nice, but there will come a moment that you will see it is all empty.

Believe what I'm saying – and if you don't, search on the internet and see how many suicides happen around the world, and you will notice how most of them happen in first-world countries, with higher net worth people. Every rule has an exception, of course, there are also lower net worth people who commit suicide, but on a much lower proportion. I am not suggesting money is a factor for suicide, but the lack of contentment with life is.

Be content with what God has given you, be grateful with your reality, whatever it is, and remember that the most beautiful and interesting stories happen when you are going through difficult and challenging moments. If you are not satisfied with what you have, try to change your mindset and your seeds, because only through contentment you will find the success that you seek.

As a great man of God once said, "If you are not satisfied with your current situation, change your seeds."

Definitely, by changing your seeds, your harvest will also change, and I hope that soon, you find what makes you feel happy, accomplished, and content with yourself. This is the great formula for success – wanting what you already have and not just wishing for what you don't, because believe me, there is much more in this world than what we truly need.

Be satisfied with what you already have, and I am sure that sooner or later, you will feel the same way you feel after a nice Sunday afternoon lunch – without any room for anything else. Truly FULL.